Through prayer...
God quenches our thirsty souls,
revives our parched hearts,
and leads us to a higher place
where peace and joy and love
will be ours forever.

Linda E. Knight

Blue Mountain Arts®

New and Best-Selling Titles

By Susan Polis Schutz:

*To My Daughter with Love
on the Important Things in Life*

To My Grandchild with Love

To My Son with Love

~

By Douglas Pagels:

*Always Remember How Special
You Are to Me*

The Next Chapter of Your Life

Required Reading for All Teenagers

Simple Thoughts

You Are One Amazing Lady

~

By Wally Amos, with Stu Glauberman:

*The Path to Success Is Paved
with Positive Thinking*

~

By Minx Boren:

Healing Is a Journey

By Marci:

Angels Are Everywhere!

Friends Are Forever

10 Simple Things to Remember

To My Daughter

To My Granddaughter

To My Mother

To My Sister

To My Son

You Are My "Once in a Lifetime"

~

By Debra DiPietro:

Short Morning Prayers

~

By Carol Wiseman:

Emerging from the Heartache of Loss

~

By Latesha Randall:

The To-Be List

~

By Dr. Preston C. VanLoon:

The Path to Forgiveness

Anthologies:

A Daybook of Positive Thinking

Dream Big, Stay Positive, and Believe in Yourself

God Is Always Watching Over You

The Love Between a Mother and Daughter Is Forever

Nothing Fills the Heart with Joy like a Grandson

The Power of Prayer

A Son Is Life's Greatest Gift

There Is Nothing Sweeter in Life Than a Granddaughter

There Is So Much to Love About You... Daughter

Think Positive Thoughts Every Day

Words Every Woman Should Remember

You Are Stronger Than You Know

The Power of Prayer

of

Wisdom, inspiration, and
comforting reminders
about the life-changing
power of prayer

Edited by Becky McKay

Blue Mountain Press™
Boulder, Colorado

We gratefully acknowledge the permission granted by the following authors, publishers, and authors' representatives to reprint poems or excerpts in this publication: Susan Polis Schutz for "I am very thankful...." Copyright © 1990 by Stephen Schutz and Susan Polis Schutz. All rights reserved. Dutton, an imprint of Penguin Publishing Group, a division of Penguin Random House LLC, for "Prayer is awe, intimacy, struggle..." from PRAYER: EXPERIENCING AWE AND INTIMACY WITH GOD by Timothy Keller. Copyright © 2014 by Timothy Keller. All rights reserved. Lisa Mae Huddleston for "A prayer spoken from...." Copyright © 2021 by Lisa Mae Huddleston. All rights reserved. WaterBrook Multnomah, an imprint of Random House, a division of Penguin Random House LLC, for "To walk with God..." from A QUIET PLACE IN A CRAZY WORLD: DRAWING NEAR TO GOD THROUGH PRAYER AND PRAISE by Joni Eareckson Tada. Copyright © 1993 by Joni Eareckson Tada. All rights reserved. Joyce Mehl for "Prayer should be a lifestyle..." from JUST IN CASE I CAN'T BE THERE by Ron Mehl. Copyright © 1999 by Ron Mehl. All rights reserved. Bonnie McKernan for "The more we pray..." from "Seven Steps to Strengthen Prayer," posted on *desiringGod*, January 2, 2017, https://www.desiringgod.org/articles/seven-steps-to-strengthen-prayer. Copyright © 2017 by Bonnie McKernan. All rights reserved. Zondervan, www.zondervan.com, an imprint of HarperCollins Christian Publishing, for "The morning offers a chance..." and "Why pray?" from PRAYER: DOES IT MAKE ANY DIFFERENCE? by Philip Yancey. Copyright © 2006 by Philip D. Yancey. And for "God smiles when we praise..." from THE PURPOSE DRIVEN® LIFE by Rick Warren. Copyright © 2002 by Rick Warren. All rights reserved. Scripture taken from the Holy Bible, New International Version®, NIV®. Copyright © 1973, 1978, 1984, 2011 by Biblica, Inc.™ Used by permission of Zondervan. All rights reserved. The "NIV" and "New International Version" are trademarks registered in the United States Patent and Trademark Office by Biblica, Inc.™ Franciscan Media for "Good morning, Lord!" from "Talking to God: Morning Prayers" by Julie Cragon, *franciscan media*, April 25, 2018, https://blog.franciscanmedia.org/franciscan-spirit/talking-to-god-morning-prayers. Copyright © 2018 by Franciscan Media. All rights reserved. Farrar, Straus and Giroux, a division of Macmillan Publishers, for "We do not pray for the sake..." from THOUGHTS IN SOLITUDE by Thomas Merton. Copyright © 1956, 1958 by The Abbey of Our Lady of Gethsemani. All rights reserved. LifeWay Christian Resources for "Certainly there's wisdom in..." from THE BATTLE PLAN FOR PRAYER: FROM BASIC TRAINING TO TARGETED STRATEGIES by Stephen and Alex Kendrick, published by B&H Publishing Group. Copyright © 2015 by Kendrick Brothers, LLC. All rights reserved.

Acknowledgments are continued on the last page.

Library of Congress Control Number: 2020946250
ISBN: 978-1-68088-356-5

and Blue Mountain Press are registered in U.S. Patent and Trademark Office. Certain trademarks are used under license.

Printed in China.
First Printing: 2021

This book is printed on recycled paper.

This book is printed on paper that has been specially produced to be acid free (neutral pH) and contains no groundwood or unbleached pulp. It conforms with the requirements of the American National Standards Institute, Inc., so as to ensure that this book will last and be enjoyed by future generations.

Blue Mountain Arts, Inc.
P.O. Box 4549, Boulder, Colorado 80306

Contents
(Authors listed in order of first appearance)

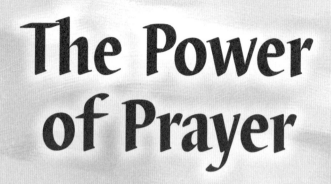

The Power of Prayer

Having prayer in your life means that you have peace and comfort in your heart as you walk down any pathway your life has to offer.

It means you can talk to a caring and compassionate Father who always has the time to listen and who never fails to understand the depths of your soul.

Having prayer in your life means having the assurance that nothing can ever come your way that you and God, united together, cannot deal with and ultimately overcome. He has His hand in everything, and things will always work out for your good.

When you pray, you can be assured, with no uncertainty, that you will be given the strength to endure anything that happens to you, and you will become a better person.

➢ Cathy Beddow Keener

Prayer is awe, intimacy, struggle — yet the way to reality. There is nothing more important, or harder, or richer, or more life-altering. There is absolutely nothing so great as prayer.

Timothy Keller

Through prayer…
God quenches our thirsty souls,
revives our parched hearts,
and leads us to a higher place
where peace and joy and love
will be ours forever.

Linda E. Knight

The power of prayer is man's greatest power.

Rev. David Thomas, DD

A prayer spoken from
the deepest longings
    of the heart
always touches God

When it seems as though
everything is falling apart
and there is nothing more
    you can do,
at that very moment
stop and give thanks
that God has heard
    your prayer

Trust in your faith
even when it's hard,
    and believe
that God is moved
    by your prayer
and a miracle
    will be born

Never give up —
let yourself be awed
    by the power
of His presence
    in our lives

✐ Lisa Mae Huddleston

Getting in the Habit

Pray in the early morning
    For grace throughout the day;
We know not what temptations
    And trials may cross our way.

Pray in the gladsome noontide,
    When the day is at its best;
Pray when the night o'ertakes thee
    To Him who giveth rest.

Pray in the silent midnight,
    If wakeful hours be thine;
Pray for a heart submissive,
    That never will repine.

Pray in the hour of sorrow,
    Pray in the hour of grief;
In coming to the Father,
    Thy soul shall find relief....

Pray for the Father's guidance
    In all thy work and ways,
So shall thy days be fruitful,
    Thy life be full of praise.

— Irene Arnold

We must pray without ceasing, in every occurrence and employment of our lives — that prayer which is rather a habit of lifting up the heart to God as in a constant communication with Him.

St. Elizabeth Ann Seton

To walk with God, we must make it a practice to talk with God.

Joni Eareckson Tada

Prayer should be a lifestyle, not an event.

Ron Mehl

The more we pray, the more we want to pray. To do this, you need to build it into the rhythm of your day any way you can: set alarms, leave notes, put it in your day planner. Prayer is a practice that requires discipline and perseverance, and we should own the cost. Prayer is the greatest act of our day, and we must fight for it....

Pull away from distractions — the phone, the computer, the TV, the constant noise of modern life — and find a way to separate yourself so you can be and feel "shut in with God." It can be a challenge when you work away from home for long hours or are sharing your house from dawn to dusk with a bunch of loud and energetic children, but make it a priority. Your car on lunch break, a quiet corner in the office, a closet in between meals or feedings or naptimes, or simply the quiet of your heart if that's all you can muster. But find solitude, and pray.

— Bonnie McKernan

A Meaningful Way to Start Your Day

The morning offers a chance to plot out the day in advance, to bring before God every scheduled appointment and phone call as well as to ask God to keep me mindful of any sacred interruptions. None of us knows what any day will bring, of course, and I find it helps to request in advance a sensitivity to whatever might transpire. I need to tune in to God's work behind the scenes. As my pastor in Chicago used to pray, "God, show me what you are doing today and how I can be a part of it." Amazingly, when I preview my day in prayer, priorities will tend to rearrange themselves during the course of the day.

Philip Yancey

O God, who hast folded back the mantle of the night to clothe us in the golden glory of the day, chase from our hearts all gloomy thoughts, and make us glad with the brightness of hope, that we may effectively aspire to unwon virtues.

An Ancient Collect

In the morning, Lord, you hear my voice;
in the morning I lay my requests before you
and wait expectantly.

Psalm 5:3 (NIV)

Lord, the newness of this day
Calls me to an untried way:
Let me gladly take the road,
Give me strength to bear my load,
Thou my guide and helper be —
I will travel through with Thee.

Henry van Dyke

Good morning, Lord!
I offer to you my day,
all of my joys and my sufferings,
my cares and my concerns,
my accomplishments
and my failures.
All that I have, all that I do,
is yours.
Keep me in your care.
Guard me in my actions.
Teach me to love,
and help me to turn to you
throughout the day.
The world is filled with temptations.
As I move through my day,
keep me close.
May those I encounter
feel your loving presence.
Lord, be the work of my hands
and my heart.
Amen.

— Julie Cragon

Why Pray?

Why pray? I have asked this question almost every day... especially when God's presence seems far away and I wonder if prayer is a pious form of talking to myself. I have asked it when I read theology, wondering what use there may be in repeating what God must surely know. My conclusions will unfold only gradually, but I begin here because prayer has become for me much more than a shopping list of requests to present to God. It has become a realignment of everything. I pray to restore the truth of the universe, to gain a glimpse of the world, and of me, through the eyes of God.

In prayer I shift my point of view away from my own selfishness. I climb above timberline and look down at the speck that is myself. I gaze at the stars and recall what role I or any of us play in a universe beyond comprehension. Prayer is the act of seeing reality from God's point of view.

— Philip Yancey

We do not pray for the sake of praying, but for the sake of being heard. We do not pray in order to listen to ourselves praying but in order that God may hear us and answer us.

🖌 Thomas Merton

Be not forgetful of prayer. Every time you pray, if your prayer is sincere, there will be new feeling and new meaning in it, which will give you fresh courage, and you will understand that prayer is an education.

🖌 Fyodor Dostoevsky

Prayer is not the easy way out. Prayer is not an easy way of getting things done for us. So many people think of prayer as a kind of magic, a kind of talisman, a kind of divine Aladdin's lamp in which in some mysterious way we command the power of God to work for us.

Prayer must always remain quite ineffective, unless we do everything we can to make our own prayers come true. It is a basic rule of prayer that God will never do for us what we can do for ourselves. Prayer does not do things for us; it enables us to do things for ourselves.

— William Barclay

Certainly there's wisdom in working hard and planning and trying to be personally responsible. Those are all good ways of attacking life. But without the addition of prayer to animate these noble qualities with the might and wisdom of God, they don't do much. Prayer is what infuses all our efforts and the genuine concerns of our hearts with God's boundless ability. Prayer is what frames our pressing, short-term issues with God's eternal perspective, showing us just how temporary — and endurable, and winnable — even our most intense battles truly are. Prayer means hope. Prayer means help. Prayer means relief. Prayer means power.

And a lot of it.

— Stephen and Alex Kendrick

God Hears
You When
You Pray

Whether your words are
shouted from the rooftops
or a mere whisper on your lips,
whether you can express yourself exactly
or don't even know what you feel in your heart,
whether your thoughts could fill a book
or your mind can only think "Please"...
God hears you when you pray.

🖎 Ali Sawyer

We speak. He listens. He speaks. We listen.
This is prayer in its purest form.... Prayer is not
a privilege for the pious, not the art of a chosen
few. Prayer is simply a heartfelt conversation
between God and His child. My friend, He wants
to talk with you. Even now, as you read these
words, He taps at the door. Open it. Welcome
Him in. Let the conversation begin.

🖎 Max Lucado

Believe that God
hears you when you pray
and responds when
you call on Him.

Share with Him your feelings
and remember that He said,
"Be not afraid.
I am with you
and I will always be.
Do not fret or have any anxiety
about anything."
Don't forget to praise Him
and honor Him with your trust,
your confidence,
and your gratitude.

God has said
He wants you to have
the desires of your heart,
that He loves you
and wants you to have
an abundant life.
Trust in the fact
that He's as good
as His word.
Rest in the attitude
that all things
will work for your good,
and believe it.

— Donna Fargo

Prayers for Letting Your Best Self Shine

Lord, make me an instrument of Thy peace;
Where hate rules, let me bring love,
Where malice, forgiveness,
Where disputes, reconciliation,
Where error, truth,
Where doubt, belief,
Where despair, hope,
Where darkness, Thy light,
Where sorrow, joy!
O Master, let me strive more to comfort others
    than to be comforted,
To understand others than to be understood,
To love others, more than to be loved!

St. Francis of Assisi

Grant me, O Lord my God,
a mind to know you,
a heart to seek you,
wisdom to find you,
conduct pleasing to you,
faithful perseverance in waiting for you,
and a hope of finally embracing you.

St. Thomas Aquinas

Let me do my work each day;
and if the darkened hours
of despair overcome me,
may I not forget the strength
that comforted me in the
desolation of other times.

May I still remember the bright
hours that found me walking
over the silent hills of my childhood,
or dreaming on the
margin of the quiet river,
when a light glowed within me,
and I promised my God
to have courage amid the
tempests of the changing years.

Spare me from bitterness
and the sharp passions of
unguarded moments.
May I not forget that poverty
and riches are of the spirit.
Though the world knows me not,
may my thoughts and actions
be such as shall keep me
friendly with myself.

Lift my eyes from the earth,
and let me not forget
the uses of the stars.
Forbid that I should judge others
lest I condemn myself.
Let me not follow
the clamor of the world,
but walk calmly in the path.

Give me a few friends
who love me for what I am;
and keep ever burning
before my vagrant steps
the kindly light of hope.

And though age and
infirmity overtake me,
and I come not within sight
of the castle of my dreams,
teach me still to be thankful for life,
and for time's olden memories
that are good and sweet;
and may the evening's twilight
find me gentle still.

— Max Ehrmann

Talk with God

A conversation with God has a way
    of putting things in perspective.
He often helps us change our attitude,
    find a solution, or see the humor.
God shows us what our talents
    and gifts are
and how to put them to use for our
    success and peace of mind.
God reminds us that mistakes and failures
    are okay;
He helps us learn from them and gives us
    the confidence to go on.

Life can be tough with all its challenges
    and problems —
we get tired and fed up, and sometimes
    we feel overwhelmed —
but it really isn't all that difficult
    when you have God...
That's when life is as simple
    as a prayer.

— Barbara Cage

Seek God's wisdom
   and guidance
in everything you do or say —
not just in times of trouble
   or sorrow.

God hears your voice
in the shadows of life
   and will give you peace,
but God is also found
in the moments of
   joy and happiness
that can fill your heart and
   make you smile.

No matter what is happening,
    talk to God.
Share what's in your heart,
or ask to be shown the way.
Pray for strength of purpose
and the willingness to surrender.
Whether your simple prayer is
a thank-you or a cry for help,
    it is heard,
and no whisper is ever turned aside.

Just keep the conversation going.
God will always listen.
That is His promise and
    that is our comfort.
                    ◄ Linda Hersey

Ask for What You Need

When I pray, which I do many times a day,
I pray for a lot of things. I ask for health and
happiness for my friends and for their children.
This is okay to do, to ask God to help them
have a sense of peace and for them to feel the
love of God. I pray for our leaders to act in
the common good, or at least the common
slightly better. I pray that aid and comfort be
rushed to people after catastrophes, natural
and man-made. It is also okay to ask that my
cat have an easy death. Some of my friends'
kids are broken and the kids' parents are living
in that, and other friends' marriages are broken,
and every family I love has serious problems
involving someone's health or finances. But we
can be big in prayer, and trust that God won't
mind if we pray about the cat.

— Anne Lamott

Met a man today. Man I had seen many times before. Just sitting. With his legs crossed, hands knotted together, head hanging, hat down, and collar up. A daily fixture on the stone bench across from the children's fountain on the town green. Asleep, I think. But his lips are moving — very carefully moving. An ordinary average-middle kind of man. Size, age, clothes, condition — all ordinary average-middle. From one to two each day he sat — undisturbed by dogs, children, buses, laughter, rain, or cold. He sat. Saying something to himself, maybe. Daily.

So I asked him. One day I had to ask him. Asked him was he all right (which meant, "What's going on, buddy?").

And you know what he said? Said he was praying. Praying. Not that praying is so strange, but he said he was praying the alphabet. Just reciting the alphabet over and over for an hour each day, leaving it to Almighty God to arrange the letters into the proper words of a proper prayer. What was missing in words, he said, he made up for in fervor. He figured God could handle it and would understand.

Robert Fulghum

A Prayer for the Ones I Love

I pray that your faith will always stay strong and bravely take you through every crisis, that hope will always blaze inside you — even when life seems bleakest — and that peace will fill your mind, heart, and spirit with every breath you take.

I pray that love will hold you close with each new day and remind you that you are never alone. I pray that joy will always come your way, so that you will experience life with delight. I pray that your kindnesses will shine in the smiles of the people whose lives you've touched.

I pray that your confidence will always be reborn whenever you take a nasty fall — and that you'll stand tall when others don't believe in your dreams, passions, and beliefs.

I pray that healing will come to you completely when you are injured — physically or emotionally — and that family and friends who love and support you will help you recover much sooner.

I pray that forgiveness will heal your heart when others cause you distress, that you'll know you are worthy of happiness and success, and that you'll be blessed with a sunny mind, heart, and attitude. I pray you will always keep close to your goals and stay focused on reaching for the stars you choose. And I pray you know I will always love you.

— Jacqueline Schiff

Lord, Bless My Mother...

Dear Lord, today I turn to you to give you thanks for my mother. With your own gift of life, she bore me in her womb and gave me life. She tenderly, patiently cared for me and taught me to walk and talk. She read to me and made me laugh. No one delighted in my successes more; no one could comfort me better in my failures. I am so grateful for how she mothered me and mentored me, and even disciplined me.

Please bless her, Lord, and comfort her. Help her loving heart to continue to love and give of herself to others. Strengthen her when she is down, and give her hope when she is discouraged.

Most of all, Lord... give my mother the graces she most needs and desires today.

— Creighton University

...and Father

Father in heaven, I thank you for my father on earth. He is one of the greatest gifts you have ever given me. Lord, bless my dad in a special way. I ask for your continued care throughout his life. Keep him safe from harm and grant him a healthy life. You alone know how much he means to me and all who know and love him. Bless his efforts with success and continue to reward his hardworking spirit.

Give him days filled with happiness, laughter, contentment, sunshine, and beauty. Give him the great joy of family times — moments to be treasured forever and memories that will never fade. Bless him with the gift of friends who will share whatever may come, the good times and the bad. And above all these other things, help him to always look to you for true peace, joy, comfort, and eternal love. Bless him now and forever.

✎ Cheryl Barker

Listen for His Voice

Prayer is...
Like quietly opening a door
And slipping into
The very presence of God.
There, in the stillness,
To listen for His voice,
Perhaps in petition
Or only to listen,
It matters not.
Just to be there,
In His presence,
Is prayer.

Author Unknown

There is hardly ever a complete silence in our soul. God is whispering to us wellnigh incessantly. Whenever the sounds of the world die out in the soul, or sink low, then we hear these whisperings of God. He is always whispering to us, only we do not always hear, because of the noise, hurry, and distraction which life causes as it rushes on.

🖌 Frederick William Faber

Learn that the silence
Is God's way of pausing
So that we may hear
The voice of Faith.

🖌 Corrine De Winter

Prayer is simply a conversation between you and God. God often speaks to us through prayer and quiet time. The issue is, sometimes our prayer tends to be one-sided. We tell God everything, but we don't leave room for Him to speak back to us. I'm pretty guilty of this, to be honest. But it's so important to take a few moments to simply sit in God's presence and hear what He's speaking from His heart to ours. Prayer is not just for us to pour out to God; it's also for us to receive from Him.

Shanté Grossett

Trust in His Answers

*B*e patient. Trust in God's timing. Don't take an item off the list just because you didn't achieve or receive something when you thought you should have....

Things happen when the time is right — when we're ready, when God is ready, when the world is ready.

~ Melody Beattie

*P*utting our faith in God's plan allows us to trust that the events in our lives are meant to be. It helps us to make choices that must be made and realize things are not really out of control — they are under His control. There is a peace that can be found knowing that His plan is playing out in our lives.

~ Rick Norman

I asked God for strength, that I
    might achieve —
I was made weak, that I might learn
    humbly to obey.
I asked for health, that I might
    do greater things —
I was given infirmity, that I might
    do better things.
I asked for riches, that I might be happy —
I was given poverty, that I might be wise.
I asked for power, that I might have the
    praise of men —
I was given weakness, that I might
    feel the need of God.

I asked for all things, that I might
    enjoy life —
I was given life, that I might
    enjoy all things.
I got nothing that I asked for —
    but everything I had hoped for.
Almost despite myself, my unspoken prayers
    were answered.
I am, among all people, most richly blessed!

— Author Unknown

Pray for Everyone in Your Life... and in the World

We should strive to keep our hearts open to the sufferings and wretchedness of other people, and pray continually that God may grant us that spirit of compassion, which is truly the spirit of God.

St. Vincent de Paul

God gave us one another
to teach us about love
and guide us through this world,
always available to help us forward
toward a greater understanding
and a greater sharing and giving
of love.

Regina Riddle

Father, help me to be like a refreshing
cup of cold water on a hot summer's day
to the friends you've given me. May I
contribute encouragement, comfort, wisdom,
accountability, and loyalty to our friendship.
Help me to reserve judgment and faithfully
pray for my friends as we walk together
heart to heart and hand in hand. Amen.

       ✑ Stephen Weber

Thank you for enemies, Lord, for they drive
    me back to you in prayer.
Thank you, God, for your sun that rises
    on everyone.
May it bring warmth and comfort to my
    enemies today.
Bless them, Lord. Heal the hurts in their lives
    just as you heal mine.
Give me the grace to show your love to
    them today.

       ✑ Roberta Hiday

O God, when I have food,
help me to remember the hungry;
When I have work,
help me to remember the jobless;
When I have a home,
help me to remember those
    who have no home at all;
When I am without pain,
help me to remember those who suffer,
And remembering,
help me to destroy my complacency;
bestir my compassion,
and be concerned enough to help;
By word and deed,
those who cry out for what we take for granted.
Amen.

— Samuel F. Pugh

Prayer Is...

...an uplifting of the heart; a glance toward heaven; a cry of gratitude and love, uttered equally in sorrow and in joy. In a word, it is something noble, supernatural, which expands my soul and unites it to God.

— St. Thérèse of Lisieux

...the ladder upon which the soul climbs to heaven. To get into fellowship with God, we must approach Him through prayer and make known our wants to Him.

— Ida Scott Taylor

...believing in something bigger than yourself or anything you've ever touched or known. It's telling a river or an open field that you need a little help.

— Ashley Rice

...the peace of our spirit, the stillness of our thoughts, the evenness of recollection, the seat of meditation, the rest of our cares, and the calm of our tempest.

 Jeremy Taylor

...a *privilege;* like friendship and family love and laughter, great books, great music, and great art, it is one of life's opportunities to be grasped thankfully and used gladly. The man who misses the deep meanings of prayer has not so much refused an obligation; he has robbed himself of life's supreme privilege — friendship with God.

 Harry Emerson Fosdick

Five Benefits of Prayer

Prayer can set (or change) the tone of your day
What sets the tone of your day? The frustration of a long commute to work? The pile of dishes in the sink and the never-ending loads of laundry? The mailbox full of bills and bad news? You wake up full of hope for a new day, then it inevitably hits a snag and you're sent swirling into frustration, anxiety, or worse. Starting your day in prayer will help to get your mind in the right place for a more joy-filled day.

Prayer helps you make better decisions
How often do you find yourself making poor decisions and wishing you'd acted differently? What difference would it make in your day if you instead... decided to react with calm and reasoning instead of yelling? Decided to take the time to really listen to a friend instead of rushing off to your next appointment? Decided to make a healthier choice instead of falling into old habits?

Even the small decisions in your life make a big difference, so how are you approaching them? Include God in big and small decisions and you'll find that He'll lead you to make wiser choices.

More frequent communication builds a stronger relationship

How often do you talk to your best friend? To your spouse? To your children? Probably more than once a week, right? Developing a strong relationship requires frequent communication. The more we talk to each other and have quality conversations, the better our relationship will be. The same is true with God. The more you pray and share your heart with God, the stronger and more personal your relationship will be.

Answered prayers are prayers prayed

If you aren't praying and asking for God's blessings and help, how do you expect Him to answer your prayers? He's ready and waiting to bless you with good gifts in His time and His way, but He wants you to first engage Him in prayer. If you want your prayers to be answered, pray daily and pray sincerely.

Opening your heart to God daily allows God to transform your heart

God's focus isn't results but hearts. He wants to win over your heart and move it closer to His. He may do that through answering earthly needs, or He may do that by working in your heart to shift your focus to Him. When you spend regular, frequent time in prayer, you allow God to do His work in your heart. Through prayer, He will transform your life and bring you to new joy in Him.

— Kathryn Shirey

Come As You Are

The only way to come to God is by taking off any spiritual mask. The real you has to meet the real God. He is a person.

So, instead of being frozen by your self-preoccupation, talk with God about your worries. Tell Him where you are weary. If you don't begin with where you are, then where you are will sneak in the backdoor. Your mind will wander to where you are weary.

We are often so busy and overwhelmed that when we slow down to pray, we don't know where our hearts are. We don't know what troubles us. So, oddly enough, we might have to worry before we pray. Then our prayers will make sense. They will be about our real lives.

Your heart could be, and often is, askew. That's okay. You have to begin with what is real.

— Paul E. Miller

One thing that I've learned recently is to experience God more abundantly in prayer. I should come as I am and connect with God. I don't need to pray in church lingo or with the most extravagant vocabulary. I just need to come as I am, because He loves me as I am.... There's no magical words or formula. He just wants time and relationship with me!! As a result, I've found my prayers to be more natural, vulnerable, and engaging!

🖋 Jeremy Lin

God knows you, knows you well; knows your needs, your heart, your yearnings; knows your hopes and dreams, your blessings and bandages. God knows you the way you hope a lifelong friend will eventually come to know you.... Prayer is, before and after all else, understanding that you are understood.

🖋 Paul L. Escamilla

Safe Place

I tap into relief,
when my voice calls out to you, Lord.

Eyes shut tight,
I fill the room with my clamor.
The sounds of my warfare,
build a tangible connection to you.

I'm in the spirit realm now.
I give in,
and my body sways
while my spirit leaps.

I arrive —
I arrive to the place,
where my spirit can perceive,
depths far beyond what our eyes can see.

— Maritza Mendoza

Whatever You're Facing... God Knows

When you are tired and discouraged
from fruitless efforts...
God knows how hard you have tried.
When you've cried so long
and your heart is in anguish...
God has counted your tears.
If you feel as if your life is on hold
and time has passed you by...
God is waiting with you.
When you're lonely
and your friends are too busy
even for a phone call...
God is by your side.
When you think you've tried everything
and don't know where to turn...
God has a solution.
When nothing makes sense
and you are confused or frustrated...
God has the answer.

If suddenly your outlook is brighter
and you find traces of hope...
God has whispered to you.
When things are going well
and you have much to be
thankful for...
God has blessed you.
When something joyful happens
and you are filled with awe...
God has smiled upon you.
When you have a purpose to fulfill
and a dream to follow...
God has opened your eyes
and called you by name.
Remember that wherever you are
or whatever you're facing...
God knows.

— Kelly D. Caron

A Prayer for Hard Times

God, be with me as I deal with this challenge. May I ask the right questions to get the kind of answers that will put every fear to rest. May those around me help me make the tough decisions.

May I prepare properly and do exactly what I need to do to help myself and enlist the help of others. God, help me choose life-enhancing attitudes.

May my mind be clear and alert and my feelings accurately guide me to make the right choices. May I face every negative apprehension with wisdom to put my mind at ease and my heart at peace.

May your love hold me closely and wrap me in your arms; may love's power be inside me and greet me every way I turn. May understanding calm my senses so I'm not anxious and afraid. God, be with me each minute of every day until I can look back and say... I'm stronger; I'm better. Thank you, Lord.

— Donna Fargo

With God, All Things Are Possible

With God, all things are possible
There are no boundaries within His realm
No mountains He can't move
No heart He cannot comfort

With God, there's only perfection
A great plan for your life
And peace for your pathway
All things are bright and beautiful

With God, there is a way to look beyond
    each circumstance —
To see Him lifting you
Above life's valleys
Moving your spirit to the mountaintop
Filling your heart with peace
And covering your thoughts with
    the beautiful presence of His love

With God, all things are possible

— Barbara J. Hall

You exist in a spiritual as well as a material universe. Life is large, mysterious, and miraculous. Remember that God is your source and something greater than you is at work in your life.

Instead of limiting yourself to what you can see or to past experience, open yourself to the infinite possibilities of what can be. Choose to believe that something larger than yourself is at work for you. That is the starting point for all the good things life has to offer. Trust this larger life to support and sustain you. Trust a wisdom greater than your limited knowledge to be provider and guide in all situations, for the highest good of all.

⟋ Candy Paull

Miracles can and do happen. They can come at any time. Even when things seem darkest, there is a miracle lurking nearby.

Believing in the impossible, even when the obvious is staring you in the face, produces extraordinary results. The darkest cloud produces the brightest light when the sun breaks through. Believing in the sun, even though you can't see it, is what faith is all about.

God knows when the impossible is just about to get you down, and He needs to let you know how much He cares. That's when He gives you the miracle you've been looking for. In that moment, the clouds part and the sun will come through for you.

*Rodger Austin

Keep Faith
in Your Heart

When all else fades and melts away, faith remains. Like a flower that blossoms in the midst of a storm, your faith will grow and bloom when you least expect it.

When you feel you've prayed every prayer and wished every wish, faith will knock gently and ask to be let in. Choose faith and you choose life. Choose faith and you choose courage. Choose faith and you choose to follow the urgings of your spirit, no matter what hardships are tearing at your heart.

There is no test to prove yourself worthy of faith. Simply invite her in, and you'll feel the arms of faith wrap around you and embrace you with quiet comfort. You'll rest in the knowing that faith is an unspoken prayer that will never leave your side.

— Rachel Snyder

The records of prayer's achievements are encouraging to faith, cheering to the expectations of saints, and an inspiration to all who would pray and test its value. Prayer is no mere untried theory. It is not some strange unique scheme, concocted in the brains of men and set on foot by them, an invention which has never been tried nor put to the test. Prayer is a divine arrangement in the moral government of God, designed for the benefit of men and intended as a means for furthering the interests of His cause on earth and carrying out His gracious purposes in redemption and providence. Prayer proves itself. It is susceptible of proving its virtue by those who pray. Prayer needs no proof other than its accomplishments. If any man will do His will, he shall know of the doctrine. If any man will know the virtue of prayer, if he will know what it will do, let him pray. Let him put prayer to the test.

E. M. Bounds

I know not by what methods rare,
But this I know — God answers prayer.

I know not when He sends the word
That tells us fervent prayer is heard.

I know it cometh soon or late:
Therefore, we need to pray and wait.

I know not if the blessing sought
Will come in just the guise I thought.

I leave my prayers with Him alone
Whose will is wiser than my own.

Eliza M. Hickok

Trust in your faith,
and know that because of it,
you will receive answers
to your prayers.

Susan Hickman Sater

Give Thanks
to God

Slow down every day and pray. Be very thankful, and life won't seem so hard. When you are thankful, you are never disappointed. When you are thankful, you have no time to complain about what you don't have. Look at your health, family, children, and other overlooked blessings and begin to thank God! This is what our Creator loves.

— Rev Run (Joseph Simmons)

A single grateful thought toward heaven is the most perfect prayer!

— Gotthold Lessing

God smiles when we praise and thank Him continually. Few things feel better than receiving heartfelt praise and appreciation from someone else. God loves it too. He smiles when we express our adoration and gratitude to Him.... An amazing thing happens when we offer praise and thanksgiving to God. When we give God enjoyment, our own hearts are filled with joy!

— Rick Warren

I am very thankful
that I am able to love
and that the love is returned to me

I am very thankful
that I am healthy
and that the people I love are healthy

I am very thankful
that I have dreams to follow
and goals to strive for

I am very thankful
for the beauty of nature —
magnificent mountains
the colorful leaves
the smell of flowers
the roaring of the waves
the setting sun
the rising moon

Everywhere I look
I see the wonders of nature
and I feel so proud
to be a small part of it

I am very thankful
for all the good people in the world
I am very thankful
that I have good friends

I am very thankful
to be alive
in a time when
we can make the world
a better place
to live in

— Susan Polis Schutz

Tending Your Garden

I have a neighbor who keeps a yard and beautiful gardens, and it's by watching Harriet that I've discovered the secret to gardens: hard work....

While our relationship with God is suffused with grace, it also takes a lot of hard work.

Plain and simple, there's nothing better than daily prayer. It's hard to get in the habit, I know, and easy to get out of it. My daily life is rushed and filled with important tasks. It can seem almost impossible to pray every single day for even fifteen minutes. But if I'm honest with myself, I realize how much time I devote to television, the internet, and all the other wonderful distractions of modern life. Surely I can cut back just a bit and give that time to God.

The result, I think, is a garden like Harriet's — lush, beautiful, and sustaining.

— Karen Stroup

Today I planted a spiritual garden
beneath the tree of love.
Wanting it full of compassion, health,
happiness, success, and prosperity,
I had to first ensure
there would be growth.

Clearing the weeds of discontent,
anger, and frustration,
I prepared myself through prayer
before planting the seeds of
faith, belief, and trust
to bring forth the flowers
of my heart's desire.

Daily will I tend my garden.
I will nurture it with patience,
constantly guard against uncertainty,
doubt, and disbelief,
and water with affirmations from the
well of divine right action.

While I wait for the seedlings to
take hold, grow, and multiply,
I will remain steadfast in knowing
that with God all things are possible —
including the blossoming
of the spiritual garden
planted deep within my soul.

— Doris K. Reed

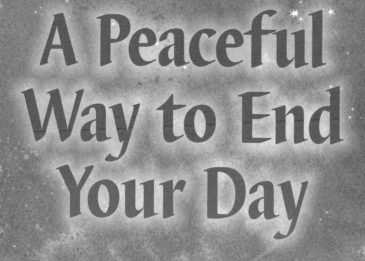

A Peaceful
Way to End
Your Day

How we end our day is just as important as how we start it. I've found that a great practice to calm your heart, relax your body, and quiet your mind at bedtime is to pray. When we converse with God about the day and share our joys, struggles, and hopes for tomorrow… we become centered, still, and ready for sleep.

— Debra DiPietro

When I look up at the night sky
and the infinite grandeur of it all,
I can't help but be awestruck.
Everything — from the tiniest speck of dust
to the most magnificent star —
is held within it, as if cradled
in God's loving embrace.
In that feeling of connection,
of togetherness,
I open my heart… and pray.

— Elspeth Jeanne

Be present, O merciful God, and protect us through the silent hours of this night so that we who are wearied by the work and the changes of this fleeting world may rest upon Thy eternal changelessness. Amen.

🖋 An Ancient Collect

Dear God, tonight as I sleep, please lift my worries and fears and in their place put faith and inspiration. Help to seed my consciousness with love and joy so I may awaken tomorrow with a deep sense of peace. Weave moments of laughter into my day and please help me to be a blessing to others. Thank you, God, for helping me to remember the beauty of this life.

🖋 Laurel Bleadon-Maffei

If I have wounded any soul today,
If I have caused one foot to go astray,
If I have walked in my own willful way —
Good Lord, forgive.

If I have uttered idle words or vain,
If I have turned aside from want or pain,
Lest I myself should suffer through the strain —
Good Lord, forgive.

If I have craved for joys that are not mine,
If I have let my wayward heart repine,
Dwelling on things of earth, not things divine —
Good Lord, forgive.

If I have been perverse, or hard, or cold,
If I have longed for shelter in Thy fold
When Thou hast given me some part to hold —
Good Lord, forgive.

C. Maud Battersby

Prayer Changes Everything

When we praise and worship God, His presence comes to dwell with us. And the most amazing thing about that is when it does, things change. Always! You can count on it. Hearts change. Situations change. Lives change. Minds change. Attitudes change.

Every time you praise God, something changes within you, or your circumstances, or in the people or situations around you. We can't see all that is being affected, but we can trust that it is, because it is impossible to touch the presence of God and there not be change. The reason for that is you are coming in contact with all that *God* is, and that will affect all that *you* are.

Praise is the prayer that changes everything.

— Stormie Omartian

Prayer is a way that our hearts
   can communicate in faith,
a way that we can ask questions
   and receive answers,
a way that we can openly express
   our feelings and concerns.
Prayer is a wonderful source of
   strength for a person,
and prayers can become even
   stronger when we turn to each
   other for support in prayer.
Lean on prayer to help you through
   difficult times,
and know with certainty what the
   power of prayer can do.

— Susan Hickman Sater

If you trust in the Lord and the power of prayer, you will overcome any feelings of doubt and fear and loneliness that people commonly feel.

🖋 Mother Teresa

More than anything, praying just helps me to concentrate and let go of things that don't matter in that moment. It gives me peace knowing I'm in good hands.

🖋 Katie Ledecky

May All Your Prayers Be Answered

May you always have a star shining over you and all the light you need to find your way. May you wake up every day and be reminded of how special you are. May all your prayers be answered and every wish come true.

May happiness grow all around you and all you need and desire find its way to you. May you see God's hands at work in everything. May you always celebrate the joys of living, knowing that more are on their way. May rainbows break through every storm and God be your refuge and strength. May the wonders of life never cease to amaze you and God's love always be greater than your needs.

May your life be one step after another leading to the stars. Whatever you encounter, may hope always be by your side. May you never underestimate the potential that lies within you or how loved you are. May the Giver of every good gift give them all to you. May you always open the window of your heart and let His love flow through you. May you always know that with God anything is possible. May He be all the hope you need and all the joy your heart can hold.

— Linda E. Knight

Acknowledgments continued...